Llamas

Victoria Blakemore

Copyright info/picture credits

Cover, Fachry Aditya Rachman/Shutterstock; Page 3, manfredrichter/Pixabay; Page 5, Perkons/Pixabay; Page 7, Capri23auto/Pixabay; Page 9, hbieser/Pixabay; Pages 10-11, pvdberg/Pixabay; Page 13, Anna/AdobeStock; Page 15, Andy Ilmberger/AdobeStock; Page 17, Alexas_Fotos/Pixabay; Page 19, manfredrichter/Pixabay; Page 21, Jeff McCollough/ AdobeStock; Page 23; ZEBULON72/Pixabay; Page 25, HO-erwin56/Pixabay; Page 27, JolEnka/Pixabay; Page 29, toddw-mac/Pixabay; Page 31, dassel/Pixabay; Page 33, Fachry Aditya Rachman/Shutterstock

Table of Contents

What Are Llamas?

Llamas are large mammals. They are related to alpacas and camels. Unlike camels, llamas do not have humps.

Llamas are **domesticated** animals. They are usually kept by people. The guanaco is a wild animal that is very similar to a llama.

Llamas are usually black, white,

tan, or brown in color. They may

also be a mix of different colors.

Size

Llamas can grow to be between five and six feet tall. Their bodies can be about four feet long from head to tail.

When fully grown, llamas can weigh between 280 and 450 pounds. Female llamas may be smaller than male llamas.

Llama feet have two soft pads and two nails. Their feet are helpful to their habitat because they do not damage the plants as much as hooves do.

Llama blood is very rich in **hemoglobin**. This allows them to survive in high-altitude areas where there is less oxygen.

Llamas have a long face. Their bottom teeth often stick out of their mouth. Their teeth are very strong so they can grind down plants.

7

Habitat

Most llamas are **domesticated**. They are found on farms and ranches. In the wild, many are found in the mountains.

Their thick fur allows them to live where it is very cold. They just need areas where there are lots of plants for them to eat.

Range

Llamas are only found in the

wild in South America.

They are mainly seen in Peru,

Argentina, Bolivia, and Chile.

Diet

Llamas are **herbivores**. They eat only plants.

Their diet is made up of leaves, grasses, and shoots. After they eat, they bring their food, or cud, back up and chew on it. This helps their three stomachs to **digest** the plants they eat.

Llamas can eat many different plants. They get most of their water from the plants they eat.

Self Defense

Llamas are able to bite and kick to defend themselves. They also spit if they feel bothered or threatened.

When llamas spit, they actually spit juices they have brought up from one of their stomachs. They can spit about fifteen feet away.

Llamas that are about to spit

flatten their ears against their

head. Then, they raise their chin

and make gurgling noises.

Communication

Llamas use mainly sound and movement to communicate. They often make humming and groaning noises. They also have an alarm call they use if they are scared.

Tail and body positions can also be used to send messages to other llamas.

Llamas move their ears and head to send messages. If a llama has its ears flattened, it may be angry and about to spit.

Movement

Llamas spend most of their time grazing, so they often move slowly. They are able to run up to about thirty miles per hour.

Llamas are able to jump several feet high. The highest llama jump on record is three feet, eight inches high.

Llamas are often seen walking

with their heads down as they

graze.

Young Llamas

Llamas usually have one baby.

Llama babies are called crias.

When they are first born, they

often weigh between twenty

and thirty pounds.

Crias are usually able to stand

and walk within about an hour

of being born.

Crias do not always have the same coat color as their parents.

Llama Life

Llamas are very social animals. They prefer to be in groups that are called herds.

They are said to be very smart. They are easy to train and learn commands very quickly. They are often shy and gentle animals. They can be very **affectionate** with people.

Herds of llamas are usually made

up of twenty or fewer llamas.

They help each other watch out

for danger and graze together.

Llama or Alpaca?

Llamas and alpacas are very similar. They are often mistaken for each other, but there are some ways to tell them apart.

Llamas are bigger than alpacas. They have a longer face and their fur is much more coarse than alpaca fur.

Alpacas have shorter faces and are smaller than llamas. Their fur is softer and more valuable than llama fur.

Population

Llamas are not **endangered**.
There are thought to be over
three million llamas in the world.
Many are **domesticated**, but
some still live in the wild.

About seventy percent of the
llama population is found in the
country of Bolivia.

Llamas often live between

fifteen and twenty years.

Llamas and People

Llamas are often kept on farms. Their fur can be **sheared** to make wool. A single llama can produce over six pounds of fleece every two years.

Many farmers keep one or two llamas in with their sheep. They help to keep the predators away.

Llamas have also been used as

pack animals. They are able to

carry over one hundred pounds.

Helping Llamas

Llamas populations in the wild are **stable**, so they are not in trouble. However, there are still ways that people help them.

Many roads in areas where llamas are found in the wild have llama crossing signs. The signs warn drivers to watch out for llamas crossing the road.

There are rescue centers that help llamas who are sick or hurt. They take care of the llamas until they can find homes for them.

Some groups focus on teaching people about llamas. They want people to learn about llamas and how they can be so **beneficial** to humans.

Glossary

Affectionate: showing love or affection

Beneficial: helpful, having a good effect

Digest: to break down food into materials that can be used and absorbed by the body

Domesticated: animals that are kept by people, not in the wild

Endangered: at risk of becoming extinct

Hemoglobin: the protein in red blood cells that carries oxygen to parts of the body

Herbivore: an animal that eats only plants

Sheared: when the fur of sheep or llamas is cut off to make wool

Stable: not changing

About the Author

Victoria Blakemore is a first grade

teacher in Southwest Florida with a

passion for reading.

You can visit her at

www.elementaryexplorers.com

Also in This Series

Elementary Explorers	Elementary Explorers	Elementary Explorers	Elementary Explorers	Elementary Explorers	Elementary Explorers	Elementary Explorers
Gray Wolves	Sloths	Flamingos	Camels	Koalas	Honey Bees	Pandas
Pangolins	White-Tailed Deer	Orcas	Giraffes	Corn	Meerkats	Echidnas
Walruses	Raccoons	Bald Eagles	Apples	Arctic Foxes	Red Pandas	Cassowaries
Tigers	Ladybugs	Moose	Beluga Whales	Leopards	Elephants	Jellyfish
Binturongs	Lions	Dolphins	Reindeer	Hammerhead Sharks	Hippos	Pumpkins
Peafowl	Chameleons	Florida Panthers	Aye-Ayes	Black Bears	Cheetahs	Manatees
Gingerbread	Polar Bears	Hot Chocolate	Orangutans	Coyotes	Marshmallows	Strawberries

Victoria Blakemore

Also in This Series

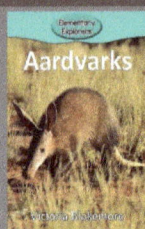

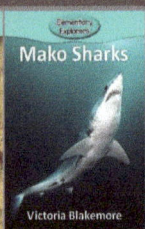

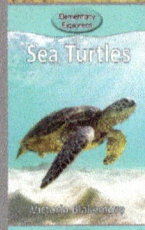

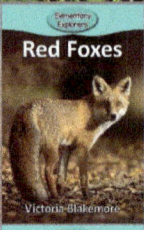

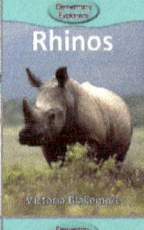

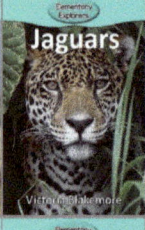

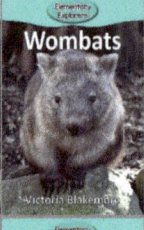

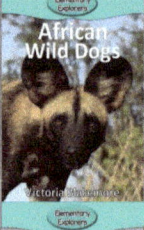

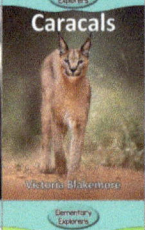

Aardvarks	Mako Sharks	Alligators	Frogs	Hedgehogs	Brown Bears	Bongos
Sea Turtles	Quokkas	Muskrats	Zebras	Red Foxes	Ring-Tailed Lemurs	Platypuses
Anteaters	Kangaroos	Rhinos	Jaguars	Wombats	Capybaras	Gorillas
Cats	Skunks	Butterflies	Dingoes	Snow Leopards	African Wild Dogs	Penguins
Whale Sharks	Wolverines	Warthogs	Caracals	Badgers	Seals	Hummingbirds
Pikas	Humpback Whales	Pumas	Lemonade	Llamas		

Victoria Blakemore

www.ingramcontent.com/pod-product-compliance
Lightning Source LLC
Chambersburg PA
CBHW051252020426

42333CB00025B/3176